Tadpole Books are published by Jump!, 5357 Penn Avenue South, Minneapolis, MN 55419, www.jumplibrary.com

Copyright ©2023 Jump. International copyright reserved in all countries. No part of this book may be reproduced in any form without written permission from the publisher.

Editor: Jenna Gleisner **Designer:** Emma Bersie **Translator:** Annette Granat
Photo Credits: Serhiy Kobyakov/Shutterstock, cover; Edjbartos/Dreamstime, 1; Svetlana Serebryakova/Shutterstock, 2tl, 6–7; Lucky Business/Shutterstock, 2ml, 12–13; AsiaVision/iStock, 2mr, 14–15; ValeryMinyaev/Shutterstock, 2tr, 4–5; Elena Elisseeva/Shutterstock, 2br, 10–11; marieclaudelemay/iStock, 2bl, 8–9; Gelpi/Shutterstock, 3; Nataliya Arzamasova/Shutterstock, 16tl; Hue Ta/Shutterstock, 16tr; Pornsawan Baipakdee/Shutterstock, 16bl; Photoongraphy/Shutterstock, 16br.

Library of Congress Cataloging-in-Publication Data
Names: Nilsen, Genevieve, author.
Title: Huelo / por Genevieve Nilsen.
Other titles: Smell. Spanish
Description: Minneapolis: Jump!, Inc., 2023.
Series: Mis sentidos | Includes index.
Audience: Ages 3–6
Identifiers: LCCN 2022035369 (print)
LCCN 2022035370 (ebook)
ISBN 9798885242547 (hardcover)
ISBN 9798885242554 (paperback)
ISBN 9798885242561 (ebook)
Subjects: LCSH: Smell—Juvenile literature.
Classification: LCC QP458 .N5618 2023 (print)
LCC QP458 (ebook)
DDC 612.8/6—dc23/eng/20220808

MIS SENTIDOS
HUELO

por Genevieve Nilsen

TABLA DE CONTENIDO

Palabras a saber 2

Huelo 3

¡Repasemos! 16

Índice 16

PALABRAS A SABER

bananas

flores

fogata

galletas

jabón

palomitas de maíz

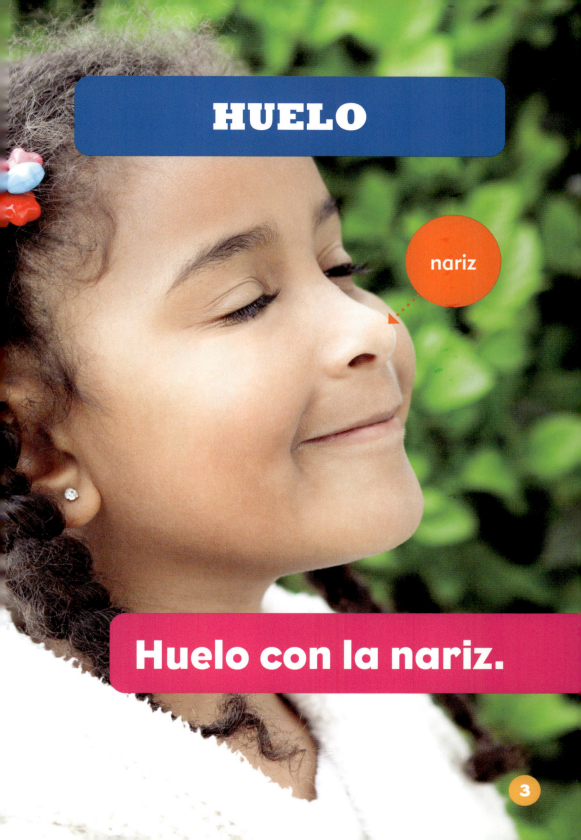

HUELO

nariz

Huelo con la nariz.

Huelo bananas.

Huelo jabón.

Huelo palomitas de maíz.

¡Huelo galletas!

¡REPASEMOS!

Usamos la nariz para oler. Mira las cosas abajo. ¿Has olido alguna de ellas antes? ¿Qué es lo que más te gusta oler?

ÍNDICE

bananas 7
flores 5
fogata 13
galletas 15

huelo 3, 5, 7, 9, 11, 13, 15
jabón 9
nariz 3
palomitas de maíz 11